DIY Paper F

Easy-to-Make and Gorgeous Paper Flowers You Can Make at Home

Harry Choi

Copyright © 2020 **Harry Choi**

All rights reserved.

ISBN: 9798664314656

DEDICATION

The author and publisher have provided this e-book to you for your personal use only. You may not make this e-book publicly available in any way. Copyright infringement is against the law. If you believe the copy of this e-book you are reading infringes on the author's copyright, please notify the publisher at: https://us.macmillan.com/piracy

Contents

Nasturtium Wreath 1

Paper Plate Flowers 12

Morning Glories 17

Coffee Filter Flowers 21

Giant Crepe Paper Roses 25

Dahlia Paper Flower Wall 38

Hyacinth Flowers 43

Persimmon Paper Roses 51

Tissue Paper Poppy Magnets 56

DIY Paper Flowers

Nasturtium Wreath

You'll Need:

TOOLS

Pliers

Toothpick

Scissors

Bamboo skewer

PAPER

60gsm crepe paper strip in light green

Double-sided crepe paper in orange/tangerine

Double-sided crepe paper in olive/moss green

OTHER MATERIALS

18-gauge wire

Parafilm tape

PVA glue

22-gauge wire

Flower templates – click here to download

Red marker

NOTE Dimensions are height x length, and paper grain is vertical

Insructions

STEM

1. Cut three pieces of 18-gauge wire, each 25 cm (10 in) long. Bunch them together and wrap the entire length of the stem with parafilm

tape. Wrap the stem with light-green paper strip, securing with PVA glue.

LARGE FLOWERS

2. Cut one 11 cm (4¼ in) piece of 22-gauge wire. Wrap the entire length of the stem with light-green paper strip, securing with PVA glue.

3. Using orange/tangerine double-sided paper, cut five petals using template A. With the orange side facing up, brush the edge of the red marker against the petals to colour. Curl each petal outwards, then ruffle the middle of the top edge.

DIY Paper Flowers

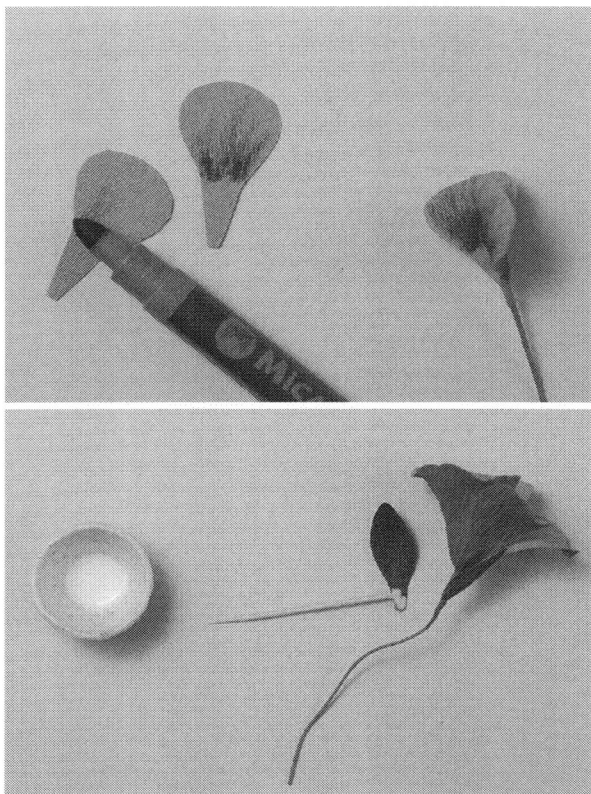

4. Using PVA glue, attach the bottom 1 cm (½ in) of each petal to one end of the stem.

5. Using olive/moss-green double-sided paper, cut two sepals with template B. With the olive side facing up, cup both sepals.

6. Using PVA glue, attach each sepal to the stem, 1–2 cm (½–¾ in) below the base of the flower. Make sure the sepals are opposite each other, with the moss-green sides facing outwards. Cover the base of the sepals with light-green paper strip.

7. Repeat steps 2–6 to make two more large flowers.

SMALL FLOWERS

8. Cut one 13 cm (5 in) piece of 22-gauge wire. Wrap the entire length of the stem with light-green paper strip, securing with PVA glue.

9. Using orange/tangerine double-sided paper, cut four petals with template C. With the orange side facing up, brush the edge of the red marker against the petals to colour. Curl each petal outwards.

10. Using PVA glue, attach the bottom 1 cm (½ in) of each petal to one end of the stem.

11. Using olive/moss-green double-sided paper, cut two sepals with template B. With the olive side facing up, cup both sepals.

12. Using PVA glue, attach each sepal to the stem, 1–2 cm (½–¾ in) below the base of the flower. Make sure the sepals are opposite each other, with the moss-green sides facing outwards. Cover the base of the sepals with light-green paper strip.

13. Repeat steps 8–12 to make two more small flowers.

LARGE LEAVES

14. Cut one 17 cm (6¾ in) piece of 22-gauge wire. Wrap the entire length of the stem with light-green paper strip, securing with PVA glue.

15. Using olive/moss-green double-sided paper, cut five fan shapes with template D. With the olive side facing up, glue the straight edges

of all five pieces together using PVA glue, overlapping by a maximum of 3 mm (⅛ in). You will end up with a round leaf. Trim the edge to neaten if necessary.

16. With the olive side still facing up, glue one end of the stems to the leaf: align the stem with one of the joins and attach it from the edge of the leaf to the centre. Allow to dry.

17. Bend the stem at the centre of the leaf to make a right angle.

18. Repeat steps 14–17 to make two more large leaves.

SMALL LEAVES

19. Cut one 9 cm (3½ in) piece of 22-gauge wire. Wrap the entire length of the stem with light-green paper strip, securing with PVA glue.

20. Using olive/moss-green double-sided paper, cut three fan shapes with template E. With the olive side facing up, glue the straight edges of all three pieces together using PVA glue, overlapping by a maximum of 3 mm (⅛ in). You will end up with a round leaf. Trim the edge to neaten if necessary.

21. With the olive side still facing up, glue one end of the stem to the leaf: align the stem with one of the joins and attach it from the edge of the leaf to the centre. Allow to dry.

22. Bend the stem at the centre of the leaf to make a right angle.

23. Repeat steps 19–22 to make two more small leaves.

ASSEMBLY

24. Take one of each flower and each leaf, and use PVA glue to join together the bottom 3 cm (1¼ in) of the stems. Cover the joins with light-green paper strip.

25. Repeat this process to make two more sprigs.

26. Using PVA glue, attach the first sprig firmly to one end of the main stem. Cover the join with light-green paper strip. Attach the remaining two sprigs to the main stem, leaving 8–10 cm (3–4 in) between each sprig. Cover the joins with light-green paper strip.

Finishing

27. Gently bend the stems to create a natural look.

HOW TO MAKE A NASTURTIUM WREATH

FLOWERS & FOLIAGE

2 Nasturtium vines

MATERIALS

18-gauge wire

Parafilm tape

60gsm crepe paper strip in light green

DIY Paper Flowers

PVA glue

INSRUCTIONS

1. Bunch three 45 cm (18 in) pieces of wire together and wrap them with parafilm tape. Repeat to make three more stems. Using parafilm tape, join the top half of one stem to the bottom half of another.

2. Join on the remaining stems in the same way. Bend the resulting length of wire to create a circle, joining the top half of the first stem to the bottom half of the last stem using parafilm tape.

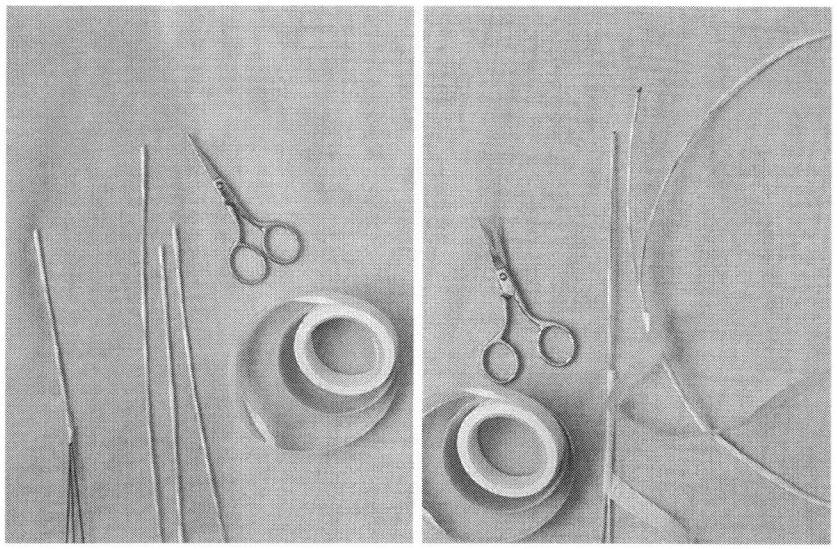

3. Wrap the entire circle with light-green paper strip and secure with PVA glue.

4. Using parafilm tape, attach the Nasturtiums to the circular frame. Cover the joins with light-green paper strip. Bend the flowers and leaves to create a natural look.

DIY Paper Flowers

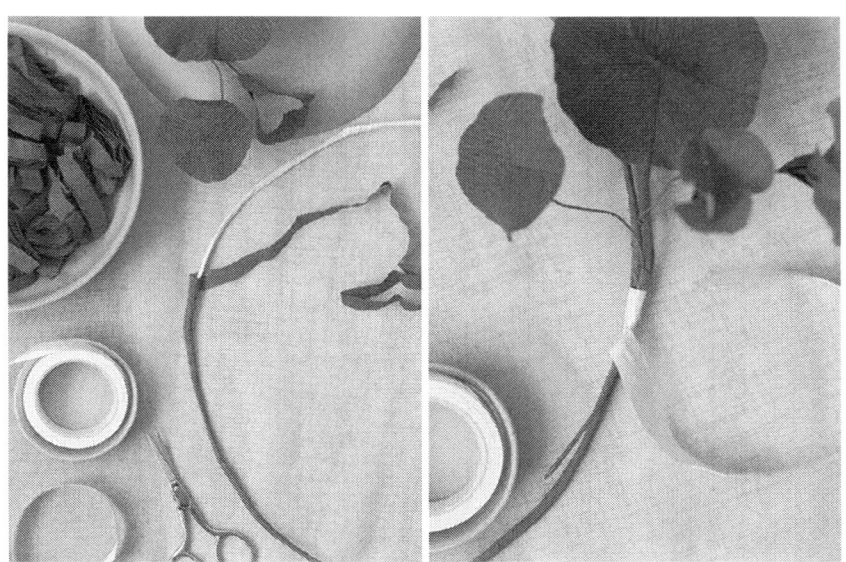

Paper Plate Flowers

You'll Need:

(5) 9-inch Paper Plates

Scissors

Hemp Cord or Metal Fasteners

Round (not beveled) Pencil

DIY Paper Flowers

Marker or Round-Handled Wooden Spoon

X-acto Knife

Hot Glue Gun

Insructions

1. Fold paper plate on dotted lines.
2. Cut paper on black dots. One side will be cut deeper than the other. You'll end up with a shamrock once the plate is unfolded.
3. Bend each curved edge around a large marker or the handle of a wooden spoon.

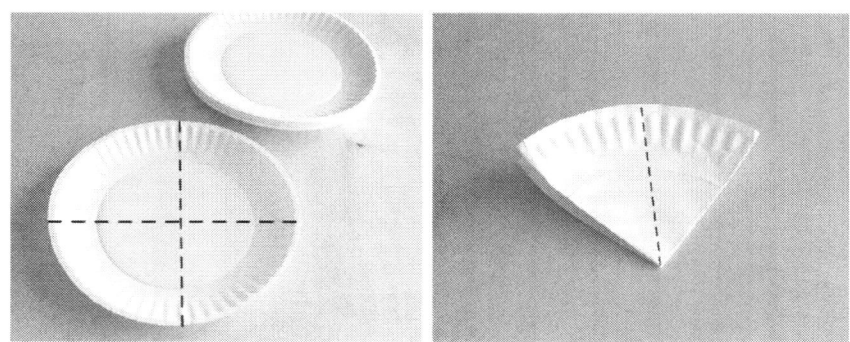

4. Lay the first plate, curved edges DOWN.
5. Fold and cut three more plates, each a little smaller than the last. Cut the edges evenly, not like the first plate. Save the cut edges! We'll use those later.
6. Use a pencil to curl the petals inward.

DIY Paper Flowers

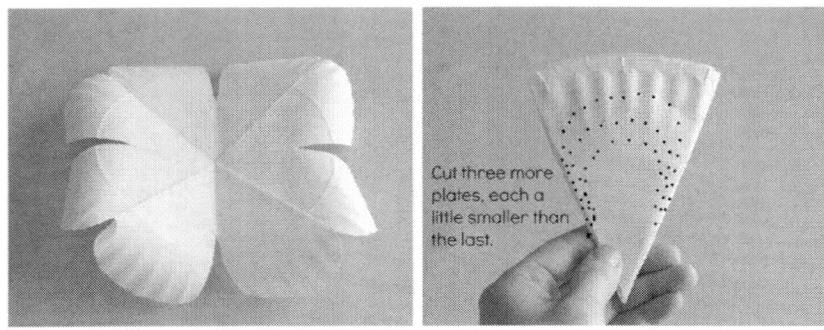

7. Keep the leftover edges folded together. Cut off the top and bottom edge.
8. Still folded together, fringe the edge. Repeat with two more leftover edges.
9. Press the fringe of ONE leftover edges against a wide marker.
10. Press the fringes of TWO leftover edges against a pencil.

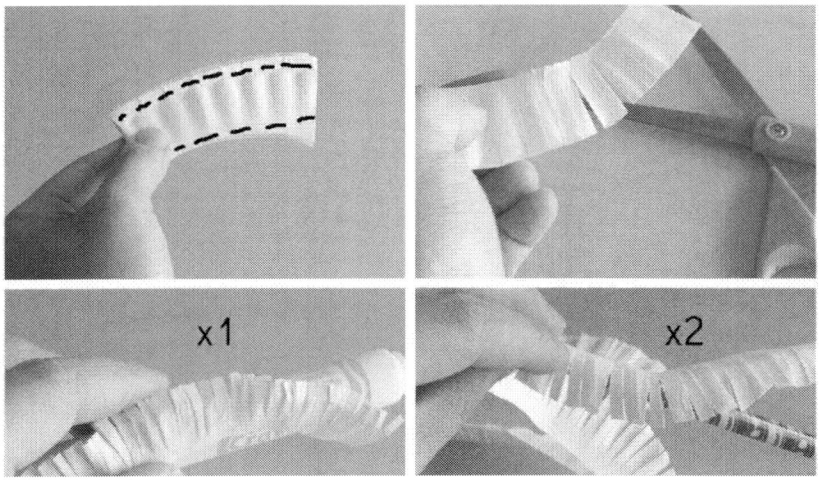

11. Use the X-acto blade to cut holes in the center of each flower.

DIY Paper Flowers

12. Place a paper fastener through all the layers
13. OR cut a three foot length of hemp cord. Fold it in half. Make a knot at the folded end. Knot again once or twice.
14. Thread the hemp through the flower petals. The knot should be in the center of the flower.
15. Tie and knot the hemp at the back of the flower.
16. Pull the hemp straight. Knot the end.
17. Cut a medium piece from the fifth plate. Sandwich the hemp between the back of the flower and the medium place of plate. Glue in place.

18. Start rolling up the pencil-curled fringe. Make sure the fringe is pointing outward.
19. Leave it slightly loose in the center so that it will fit over the hemp knot. Glue at regular intervals until you reach the end of the first fringe. Glue the end to the second fringe. Keep

DIY Paper Flowers

rolling. Glue third (marker-rolled) fringe.

20. Place hot glue all over blue areas. Press and hold together until the glue cools.
21. Decide how to layer the petals. I offset my petals (third picture below) so that it would look like a full-blown tea rose.
22. Add drops of glue between the petal layers to help keep the petals in place.

Place hot glue on blue areas.

23. I used a fan brush and watercolors to give them a pretty tinted hue.

16

Morning Glories

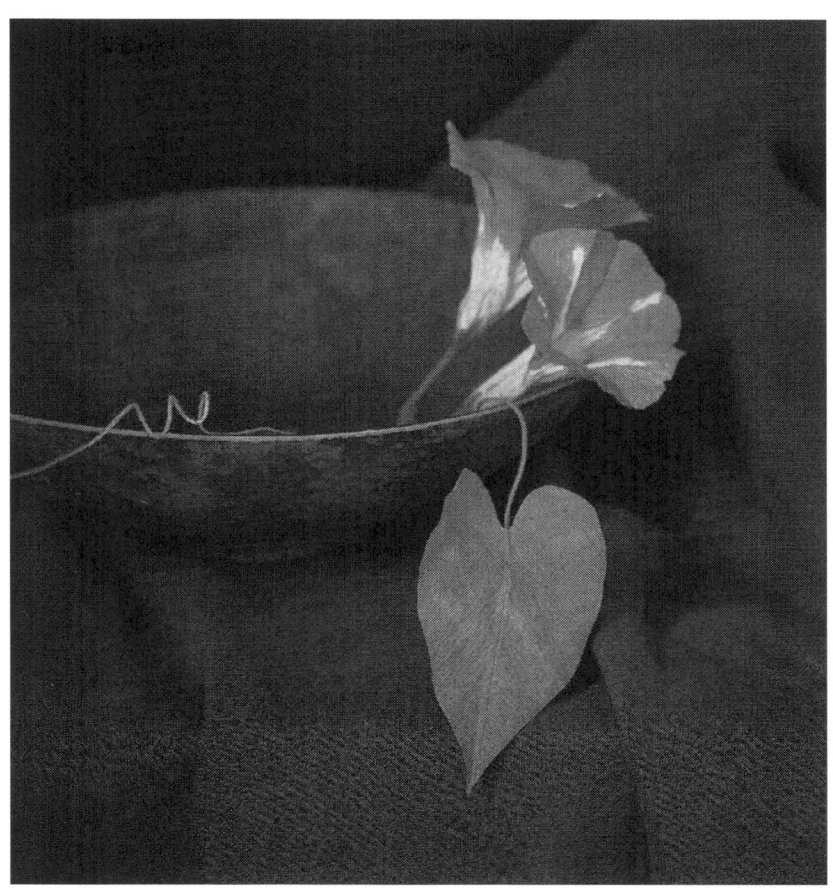

You'll Need:

Tacky glue

Hot glue

180 gram peacock blue crepe paper (also shown 100 gram iris blue, 180 gram #555 deep blue, and #600/2 sky blue ombré)

100 gram white crepe paper

60 gram #296 yellow crepe paper (optional)

Rounded paintbrush handle

Light-green floral tape

24-gauge green cloth-covered stem wire

Leaves (below)

Bleach (optional)

Small glass bowl (optional)

Round, pointed paintbrush that can be bleached (optional)

Instructions:

1. Cut five petal segments using template MG from outstretched blue crepe paper in yourdesired hue. Attach two segments together face-to-face with a line of tacky glue along one edge, starting a hair wider than 1/16" at the base and tapering to a very thin line at the top. Press together to set, then gently open the petals, turn them over and glue the back flap down from the bend in the petal to the base. Repeat with the remaining petal segments, gluing the flaps down in the same direction each time.

2. Crease the centerline of each petal segment inward, then repeat step 1 with the two unattached ends to close the flower and glue the back flap down. Insert a round-ended paintbrush and twist the

bottom tip closed below the end. Groom the top open by bending the petals back at each seam gently.

3. Trim the seam corners to round the top of the flower. Cut tiny Vs with rounded edges where the petal segments meet and at their centers. If bleaching, dip a round, pointed paintbrush in a small glass bowl of bleach, wipe off the excess, and insert into the flower's base, bleaching the bottom. Carefully extract the brush, then run the tip up the center of the back of each petal segment to ¾" below the top edge. Allow to dry. Be sure to work in a well-ventilated area. For a tricolored flower, glue small segments of finely fringed outstretched white crepe paper layered with ripped bits of thin yellow crepe paper to the inner petal surfaces before closing.

4. Wrap the top 1½" of two 2"-and one 8"-long pieces of stem wire with outstretched white crepe. Wrap the wires together with floral tape, the 2" pieces set ¾" below the 8" piece, leaving most of the white exposed. Snip the twisted bottom end from the flower and thread the wrapped wire through, aligning the tip of the wires with the bend in the petals. Secure in place with hot glue. Cut five continuous sepal points from a 5/8"-long bit of floral tape and attach at the base of the flower with tacky glue, holding in place until set. Wrap leaf and flower wires around a ¼" paintbrush handle 3 or 4 times in a few different spots to mimic the morning glory's spiraling vines.

DIY Paper Flowers

Coffee Filter Flowers

You'll Need:

Natural Coffee filters

Floral Wooden picks

Floral Wire

Needle Nose Pliars (optional)

And just a word about natural coffee filters…these little guys are GREAT! They're a beautiful, soft color right out of the package. Take one and scrunch it up …now un-scrunch and flatten it, now press your hand on the paper and just feel it. The texture is divine. There are so many things you can do with these super cheap paper filters!

Okay…let's get started!

Instructions:

1. Take a filter and fold like the first 3 photos below, until you have a cone shape…Now cut little scallops in your cone.

DIY Paper Flowers

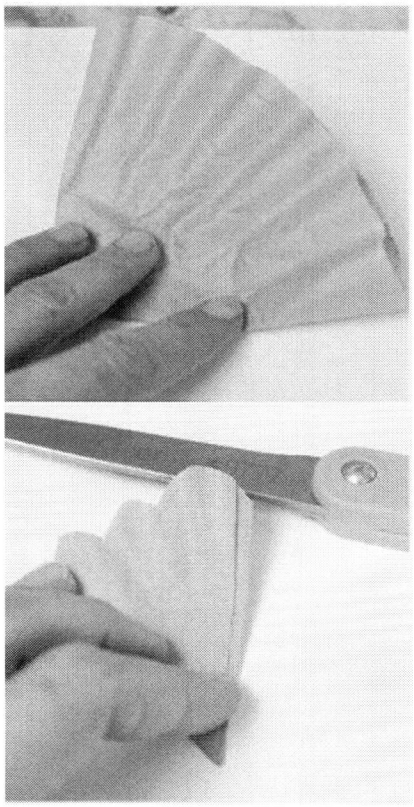

2. Do the same with 2 more filters but cut different sizes when you cut your scallops. You'll end up with a small, a medium and a large scalloped cone! Now unfold these little wonders!

DIY Paper Flowers

3. Cut a tiny tiny slit in the center of the 3 papers and insert your wooden floral pick (take off the thin copper wire from your pick before inserting-the wire is useless for this project.)
4. Pinch the papers together underneath the flower...now, turn and continue pinching...can you see your flower blooming?!
5. No, cut a section of floral wire and wrap around the pinched paper under the flower around your stem...twist to secure the wire and trim.

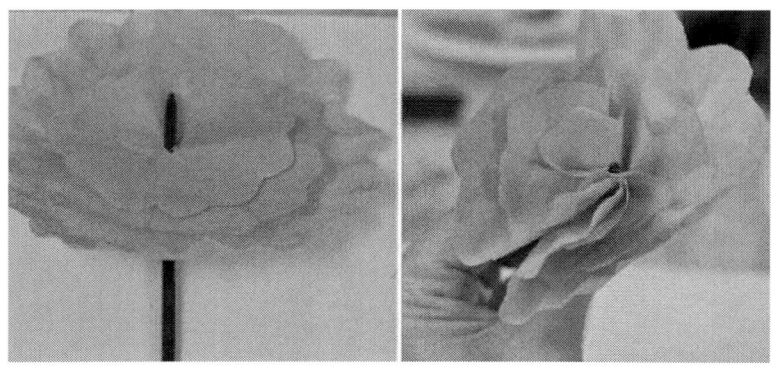

DIY Paper Flowers

Giant Crepe Paper Roses

You'll Need:

5 Small Petals

15 Heart Shaped Petals

3 Leaves

1 Calyx

2 1" Wide Crepe Paper Strips (Just cut the entire bottom off of one of your crepe paper sheets)

I recommend sacrificing a bit of paper and cutting several layers at a time (Believe me, it's for your own sanity). I folded the crepe over and over again and stapled a template to the stack. Then I cut through all the layers that way, around the outlines of the shape. I found that I could get 8 heart shape petals out of each crepe sheet, 16 small petals per sheet, 17 leaves per sheet and 12 calyx (plural!?) per sheet. You can get 10 strips of crepe out of each sheet. You can also get a few additional small petals out of your leftovers from cutting the heart shape petals.

Instructions:

1. Begin by cutting everything out as listed above. Iron the petals, as necessary, to remove creases. Then make your stem. To do this, wrap three stem wires together with floral tape. It is important to stretch the floral tape as you wrap to activate the adhesive. Keep a damp towel near you to wipe your fingers as you go, they will get sticky.

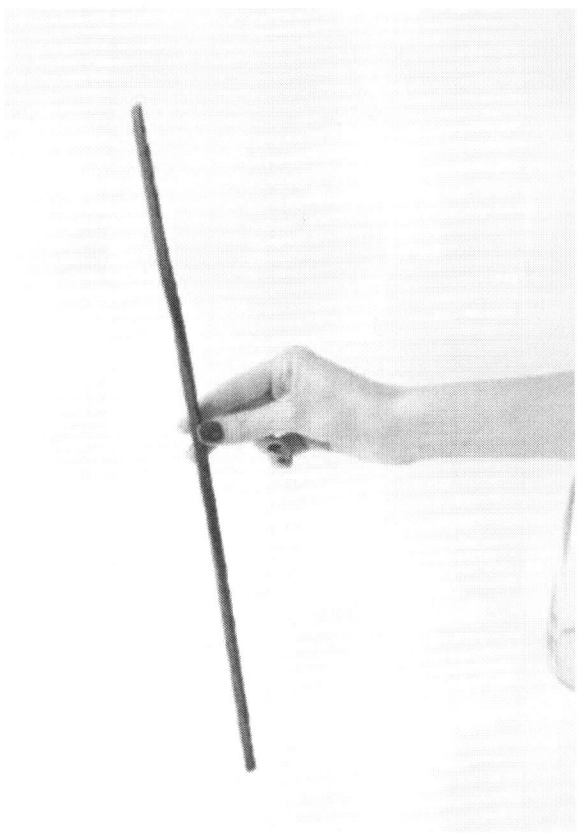

2. You'll need to shape all of your petals. To shape the small petals, start in the middle of the petal and firmly but carefully pull the crepe outwards and upwards, forming a "cupping" shape in the center of the petal. Don't be afraid to stretch the crepe! It can take it. Now you'll need to curl the top edges of your petals. Do this by wrapping the top around a pencil, while stretching the crepe slightly to avoid wrinkles, about one to one and a half times.

DIY Paper Flowers

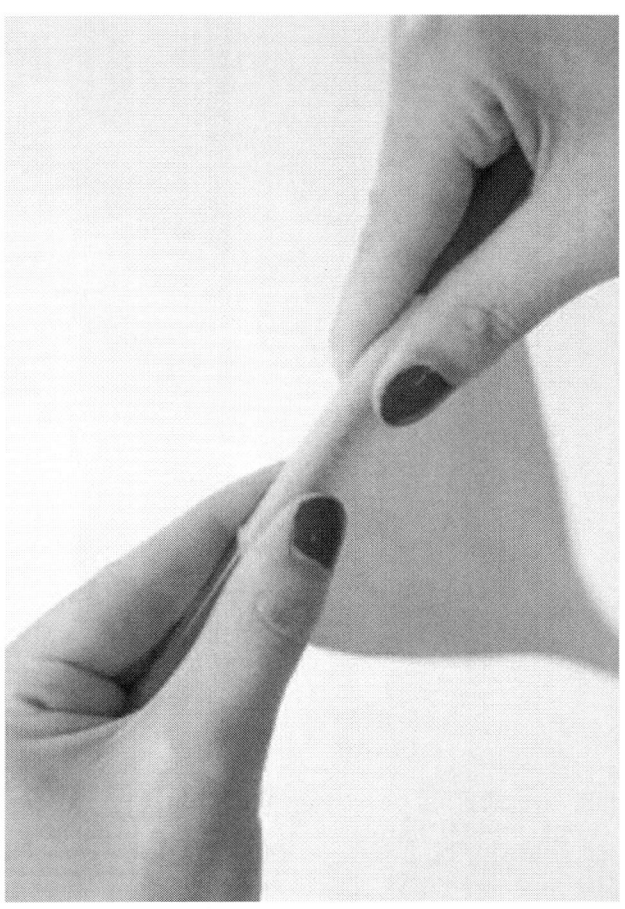

3. Do the same steps with the larger heart petals. Again, only stretch the center of the crepe, not the edges or the bottom. Curl each top-side of the heart as you did above.

DIY Paper Flowers

4. Voila! This is a tedious step but try your best to keep the shapes of your petals consistent.

5. Now you'll need to make your bud using your five small petals. Start by wrapping one petal tightly around the stem. Continue wrapping each petal around, rotating the stem each time, until you've used all five.

6. Your bud should look something like this. It is OK if your petals wrinkle, fold or bend slightly at the bottom. (Really! It is!) Now you'll need to secure your petals with your floral tape. Wrap the tape all the way down the bottom of the petal

DIY Paper Flowers

until you hit the green of the stem again, this will secure the petals in place firmly.

7. Now you'll begin adding all 15 heart petals. Add as many petals at a time as you feel comfortable. I typically tape two petals at a time until I get to the last few, then I add one at a time. Each time you add a petal you should be rotating the rose slightly so the petals are spread around the rose evenly.

8. As your working, slip your fingers inside each petal and push the petal out to form it back to shape. After each petal, or

few petals, use the floral tape to secure. Again, it is ok to have slight wrinkles and folds in the base of the petal where you are taping. Wrap the tape around and around until you hit the green of the stem again so it is secure! (This is so important.)

9. As you get to the last few petals, look at your flower from above so you can strategically place them where you think they are needed.

10. After all of your petals are secured, it's time to add the calyx to the bottom of the rose. Flip your rose upside down to do

this. Wrap your calyx piece around the stem. Fair warning: this step is awkward. It is only important for the large leaf-parts of the calyx to be flat and smooth along the flower. It is normal for the top of the calyx to NOT BE SMOOTH against the stem. (See Below) Starting on the stem wrap tape, continuing down over the calyx to secure.

11. Set your roses aside to work on the leaves. Place a hefty amount of glue down the center of your leaf and lay a single stem wire in it. Fold your leaf over the stem and pinch and press along the stem to secure the two sides of the leaves together, covering the stem. Let dry.

12. To "open" your leaves (once dry), I suggest holding on to the top of the stem on the back of the leaf and carefully bending it backwards. Now add a dot of glue to the base of your leaf to begin wrapping your stem in one of your matching crepe paper strips.

13. Wrap the crepe paper down the leaf stem just as you did with the tape on the flower's stem. You only need a dot of glue at the top and bottom, nowhere in between! Wrap tightly in a diagonal motion, stretching the crepe as you go. Secure the end with glue. Repeat all these steps with two more leaves.

DIY Paper Flowers

14. Now you'll need to temporarily secure your leaves to the flower stem. Place your leaves around the stem as desired and tape, wrapping around just a few times, just below where you're going to want your leaves to "bend." You can place your leaves as far up or down on the flower's stem as you want. Once they're secured with tape, bend the leaves far outward so you have space to work. Place a dot of glue on your calyx and begin wrapping the stem with your second strip of crepe paper. It is a little tricky at first as you'll get a bit caught up in the leaves. Just work slowly and be persistent,

tightly wrapping as you go.

15. When you hit where your leaves are taped, simply continue wrapping the crepe paper but wrap over the leaf stems as well. Then wrap all the way down to the bottom of your stem and secure with glue. I placed my leaves up higher so my stems were not all even on the bottom. I though the crepe paper disguised this well enough and the unevenness at the bottom didn't bother me. If it bother's you, you can align all your stems at the bottom, but your leaves will be significantly farther away from the flower.

Bend all your leaves as desired and you are done!!!! I truly think this is one of my favorite crafts I've made. They are just so darn pretty!

Top Tips for Making Paper Roses

1. Only shape the petals in the center! Leave the edges and the bottom points of the petal untouched.

2. Stretch the floral tape as you wrap. If you don't, the adhesive won't be activated and it won't stick very well.

3. When attaching your petals always continue wrapping the tape down to (and on to) the stem. Allowing the tape to stick the stem keeps the petals from spinning around.

4. Don't be afraid of wrinkles and folds in the bottom! The bottom of the rose is covered and it is ok for the petals to not form perfectly around the stem at their base. Seriously, this was my biggest obstacle and I almost drove myself nuts trying to make them perfect and smooth.

5. Always re-shape your petals as you work. Slip your fingers into the petal and re-"cup" it so it lays close to the previous petal. This will create a tight and secure rose.

Dahlia Paper Flower Wall

You'll Need:

Glue Gun

65-pound cardstock

Scissorsand/or cutting machine (Cricut Explore Air 2 Machine)

If you are interested in the vines I used in the photo above they can be found here. Long fern vine. Leafy vines.

DIY Paper Flowers

Instructions:

1. As I mentioned above the giant dahlia paper flower is made from 2 basic geometric shapes—a large 8 inch circle for the base and several 4.5 inch and 4 inch squares rolled into a cone shape.
2. Start with cutting out 40 of the 4.5 inch squares and 15 of the 4 inch squares. It's important to note that the final count of squares used may vary a little for everyone, but this is a good place to start.

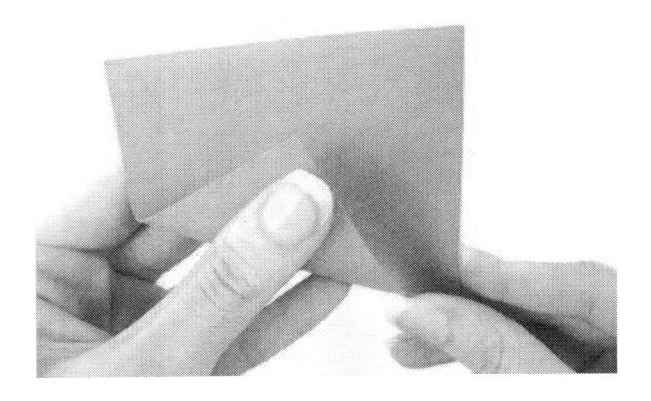

3. To form a cone, hold the square with one corner up and overlap the bottom, securing with your hot glue.

4. The 8 inch circle will be your base for gluing the cones to. If you want a variety of sizes of dahlia paper flowers you can do this by increasing or decreasing the circle base and adding or subtracting cones.

5. If you are aiming the for the ombre effect choose 3-5 shades of one colors to use progressively as you work towards the

center.

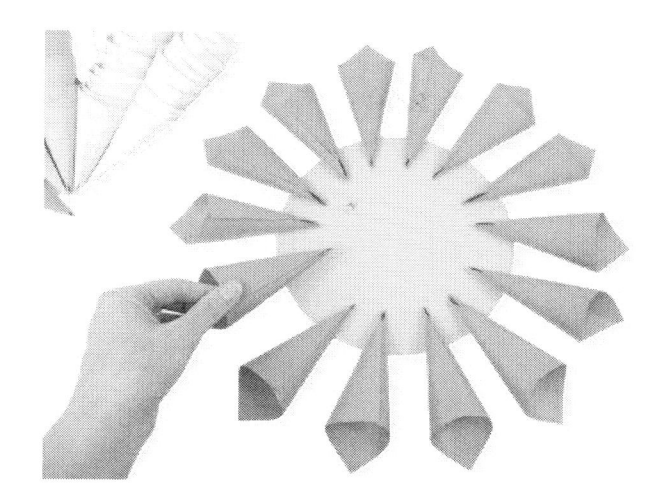

6. Beginning with your larger cones made from the 4.5 inch sqaures, glue the tips to the outer edge of the circle all the way around. Make sure to leave about a 1/2 inch or so of space between each cone.
7. Next, continue adding cones. Place the cones in the spaces we left between the first layer of cones we glued down.

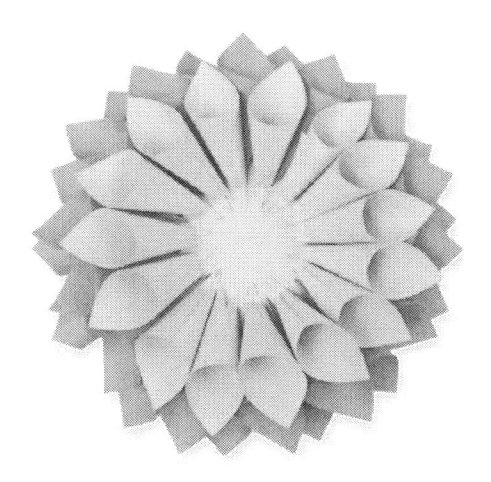

8. You would have moved on to your 4 inch cones now. Continue the pattern and keep filling in more of the dahlia cone petals.

9. Once you get down to the last half dozen or so of the cones, they will naturally bend at the tip when you glue them down. This is what you want so that the final look is a tight dahlia center. You may need to grab a thin wood dowel or pencil to press the tip down and ensure it makes good contact in the center with the glue.

Hyacinth Flowers

You'll Need:

Assorted colours of cardstock (Not too thick. Mine was 65 lbs, but thinner paper will work too)

Green construction paper (It needs to be thin)

Scissors

Ruler

Pencil

Glue Stick

Knitting Needle (optional)

Instructions:

1. Cut out a strip of cardstock paper approximately 8.5" x 2". If your paper is only 8" wide, a strip 8" x 2" wide will work too. I just made mine the length of my paper.

2. Mark 3/8" from both edges of the paper and use a pencil to lightly draw a line across the paper.
3. Using scissors (I tried an exacto knife, and scissors are waaaaaay easier), carefully snip the paper into strips that are about 1/4" wide, cutting up to the pencil line.
4. Continue cutting 1/4" strips until you've made it across the entire strip of paper.
5. Try to keep your cuts as straight and parallel as possible, but

don't panic if they aren't perfect. It won't really matter once you've swirled them up.

6. Using a knitting needle or wooden skewer, carefully roll each strip. Make sure the pencil line is on the BACK of the strip like in the photo below. You want to roll the strips away from the pencil line so it's not visible when you're done the flower.

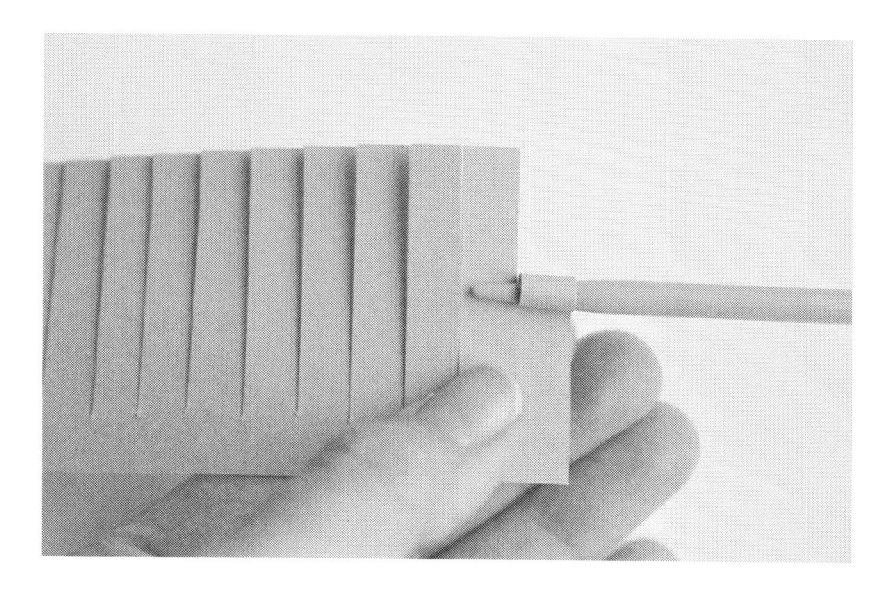

7. Roll each strip as far as it will go.
8. And continue rolling until you've rolled each piece along the entire length of the paper.

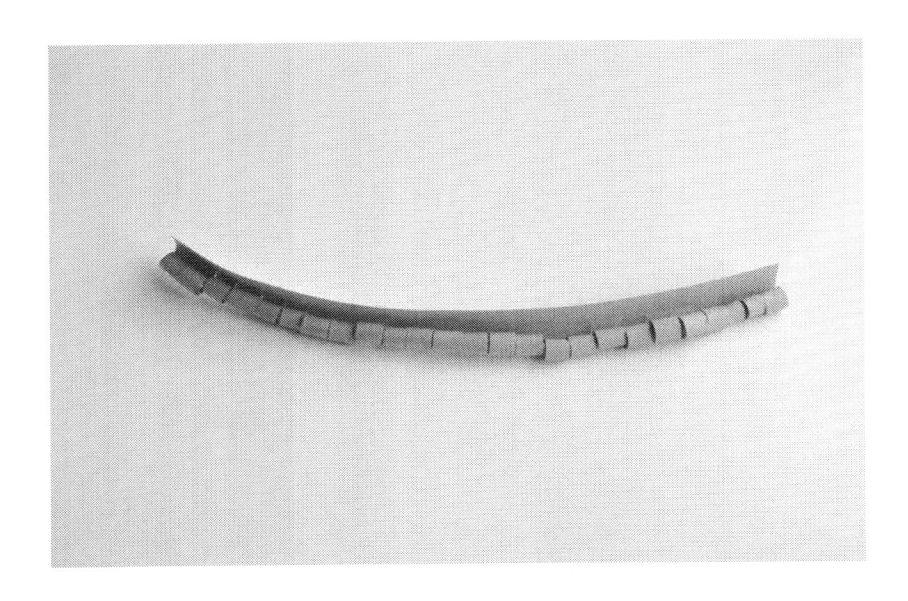

Making the Stem:

1. Next, you'll need to make the stem. Make sure you're using construction paper or another type of thin paper or you won't be able to roll it. Or if you want to save time, just use green straws as the stems.
2. Cut out a strip 2" x 8".
3. Start rolling one of the corners diagonally. Once you've gotten it started, add some glue to the paper to help keep it together.

DIY Paper Flowers

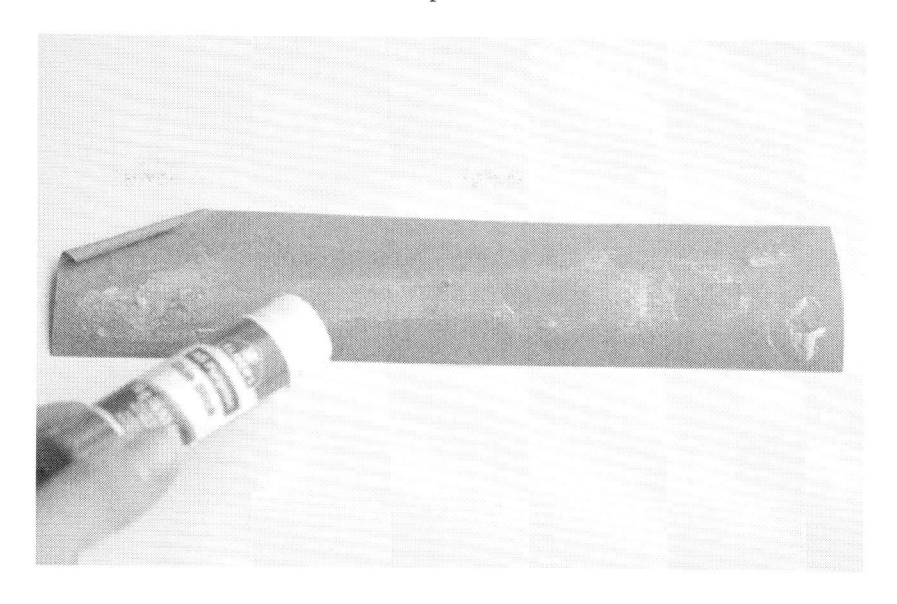

4. Keep rolling the green paper diagonally around itself to make a thin, stem-like tube.
5. When you're done, it will look something like this:

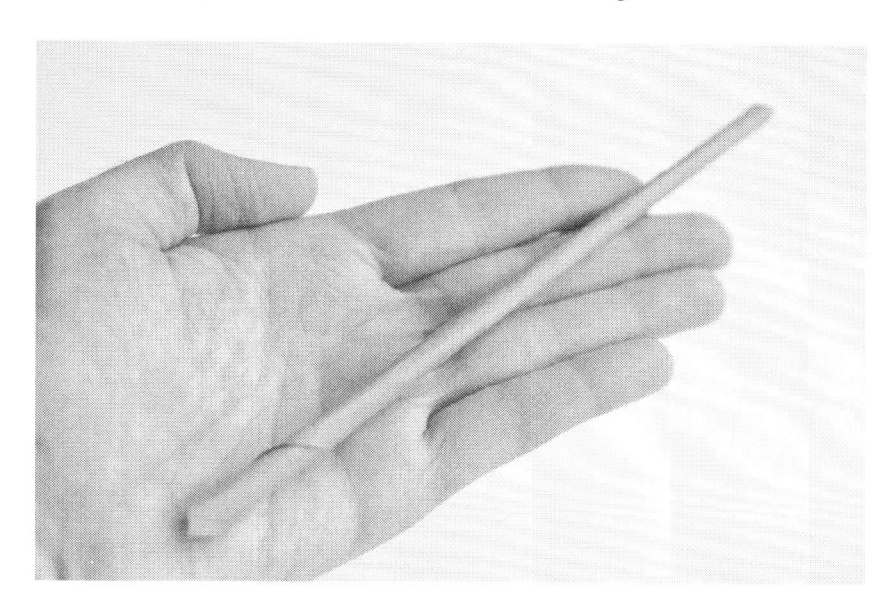

6. Adding the Flower to the Stem

7. Add some glue to the back of the swirled up paper.
8. Then place it over the thinner end of the stem with the swirls pointing up and towards the outside, like in the photo below.
9. Start wrapping the swirled up paper around the stem so that it overlaps itself as you go.

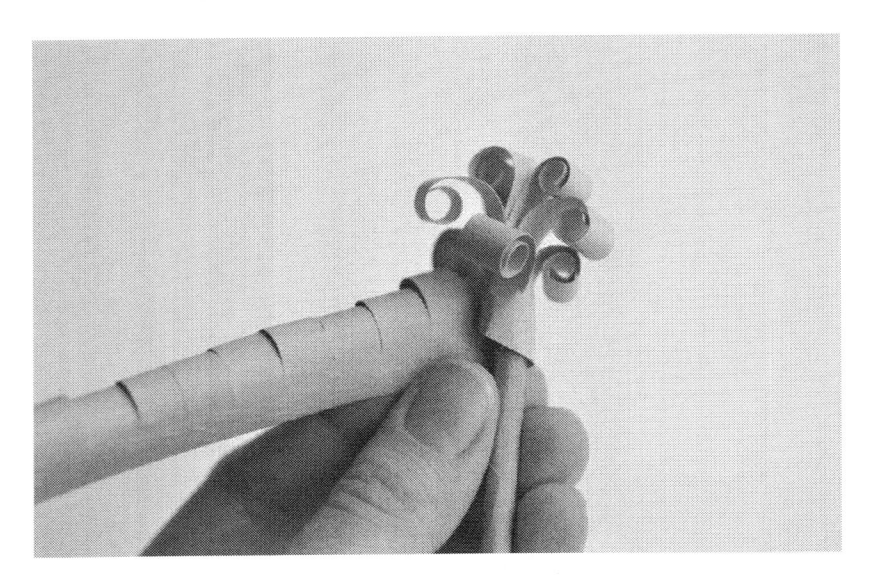

10. Try to get it as tight as you can around the stem until you reach the end of your swirled up paper strip. If you need to, add a bit of extra glue to the end to help keep it in place.

Making the Leaves

1. Next, you're going to need some leaves.
2. Cut out a piece of paper, about 2" x 3". Fold it accordion style along the long edge in roughly 1/4" sections.

3. Using sharp scissors, cut out a leaf shape, leaving about 1/2" at the bottom to give you room to glue it later.
4. Here's what my leaf shape looked like before I unfolded it:
5. And here's what it looked like after it was unfolded. You'll

end up with 3 or 4 "leaves".

6. Next, add some glue to the bottom of the leaves, and place one corner about 2" below the flower
7. Wrap it tightly around the stem as you press down the glue to keep it in place.

8. And there you have it! One paper hyacinth flower!
9. Repeat the process in different colours to make yourself a beautiful bouquet!

DIY Paper Flowers

Persimmon Paper Roses

You'll Need:

6 pieces of 8.5×11 colored cardstock

12 pieces of cloth stem wire

1/2 a bag of marble accents

Silhouette Portrait

Silhouette Portrait cutting mat

wire cutters

glue gun

a coordinating vase

ribbon for vase (optional)

spray bottle with water (optional)

Instructions:

1. Buy the 3D paper rose (Design #:11563) from the Silhouette online store. Import the file into Silhouette Studio and re-size the shape so two can fit on one 8.5×11 sheet of cardstock. Cut the file six times using all 6 pieces of 8.5×11 colored cardstock. The result is 12 flower shapes.

2. Heat up the glue gun.

3. Cut one piece of cloth stem wire to desired length. I used lengths of 9, 10 and 11 inches.

4. Add a small line of hot glue near the edge of the straight strip on

the shape. The line is only about half the length of the paper strip so that the stem wire won't show. Add the stem wire to the hot glue and fold it over to make the first turn in the rose.

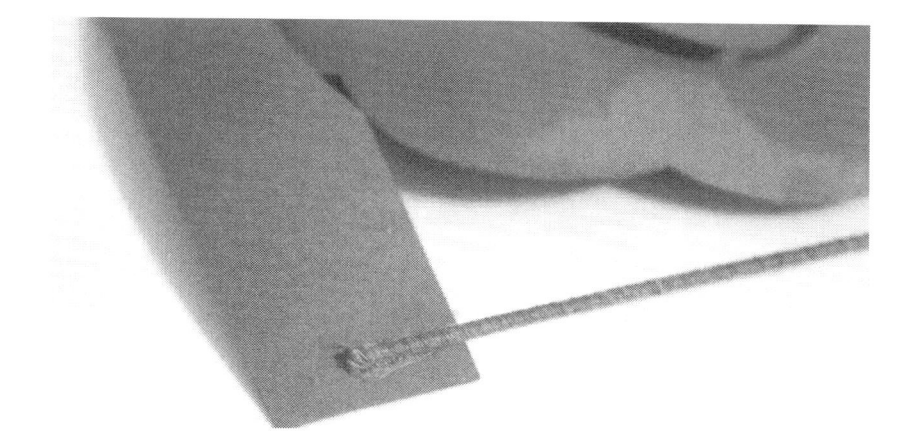

6. (Optional) Spray the shape with water so that it will bend and curl easier. This is optional but I did do one or two roses without the water spray and they were much harder to do. Beware that some of the color may bleed onto your hands. I think my fingers will be persimmon for a day or two.

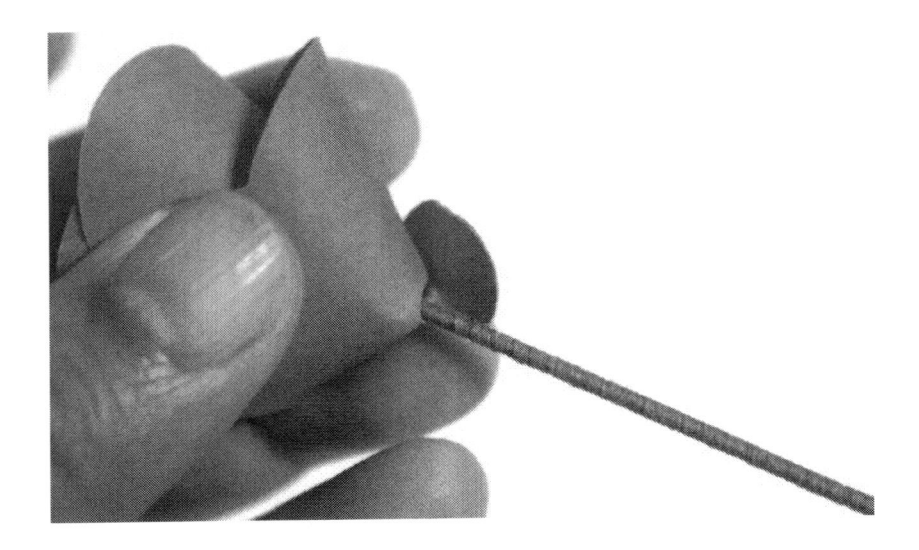

5. While holding the shape, turn the stem wire over and over again so that the paper wraps around it and the paper. When the last part of the shape has been folded around the wire, use the hot glue to secure it to the paper and to the stem. You will notice my fingers are the color of the paper in the photo below due to the color bleeding from the water spray.

You really have to play around with wrapping the rose. There were a few roses where I put hot glue on the paper as I went to hold the rose's shape but the roses turned out very tightly wound. The looser roses are a result of me letting the paper relax a little bit before I glue down the end to the stem.

6. Repeat steps 3 through 5 for all the flowers.

7. Place marble accents in the bottom of the vase to form a base for the flowers to sit on.

8. Add the flowers to the vase and arrange them. I had to position them into the marble accents at the bottom of the vase to get them to stay. When I had the flowers where I wanted them, I added more marbles in between the flower stems and that helped hold my flowers in place.

9. (Optional) Hot blue the ribbon onto the vase.

DIY Paper Flowers

Tissue Paper Poppy Magnets

You'll Need:

issue paper, any and all colors

magnets

pipe cleaners, any color works

hot glue

scissors

pencil

Instructions:

1. Begin by cutting a stack of circles: 1 stack for the flower (any amount you want) and 1 smaller stack (like 5 pieces) for the center. Poppies are known for their dark centers but you can choose whatever color you want.

2. Stack the circles, the smaller ones in the center of the larger ones, and skewer it with the pipe cleaner. Bend over the tip of the pipe cleaner to keep it from slipping out.

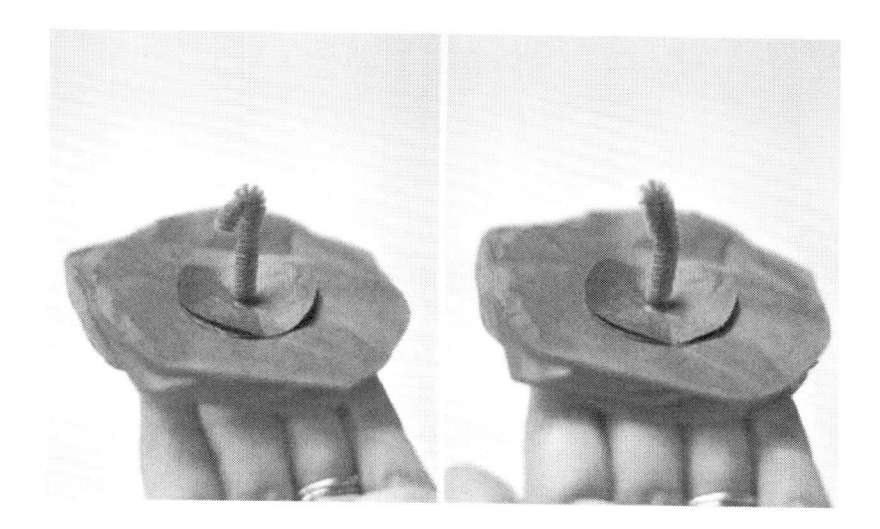

3. Pull the pipe cleaner down so the folded tip is snug in the center of the tissue stack.
4. Add a dot of glue to the pipe cleaner bump and pull the first layer of the center tissue stack up around it. The glue will hold the tissue around the pipe cleaner so it isn't visible anymore. Continue pulling the layers of tissue up and around the center, creating the cupped flower shape.

5. Trim the excess pipe cleaner. Add a dot of glue and...

add a magnet.

DIY Paper Flowers

6. After that, make lots and lots and lots of colors! And smile!
7. Take care.

Printed in Great Britain
by Amazon